YOUR KNOWLEDGE HAS VALUE

- We will publish your bachelor's and master's thesis, essays and papers

- Your own eBook and book - sold worldwide in all relevant shops

- Earn money with each sale

Upload your text at www.GRIN.com and publish for free

Bibliographic information published by the German National Library:

The German National Library lists this publication in the National Bibliography; detailed bibliographic data are available on the Internet at http://dnb.dnb.de .

This book is copyright material and must not be copied, reproduced, transferred, distributed, leased, licensed or publicly performed or used in any way except as specifically permitted in writing by the publishers, as allowed under the terms and conditions under which it was purchased or as strictly permitted by applicable copyright law. Any unauthorized distribution or use of this text may be a direct infringement of the author s and publisher s rights and those responsible may be liable in law accordingly.

Imprint:

Copyright © 2016 GRIN Verlag
Print and binding: Books on Demand GmbH, Norderstedt Germany
ISBN: 9783668638082

This book at GRIN:

https://www.grin.com/document/411977

Jan-David Franke

Aus der Reihe: e-fellows.net stipendiaten-wissen

e-fellows.net (Hrsg.)

Band 2671

Have Southern social movements achieved power and voice? Whom do they represent?

GRIN Verlag

GRIN - Your knowledge has value

Since its foundation in 1998, GRIN has specialized in publishing academic texts by students, college teachers and other academics as e-book and printed book. The website www.grin.com is an ideal platform for presenting term papers, final papers, scientific essays, dissertations and specialist books.

Visit us on the internet:

http://www.grin.com/

http://www.facebook.com/grincom

http://www.twitter.com/grin_com

W5Q2. Have Southern social movements achieved power and voice? Whom do they represent?
Jan-David Franke

What do the Ghanaian Convention People's Party, the Narmada Bachao Andolan, and the Occupy movement have in common? Answer: they all are (Southern) social movements inhabiting and representing the subaltern. What is more, they are indicative of how the dynamics in which such social movements are embedded and to which they respond have changed and of the subsequent transformative impact that has had on counter-hegemonic social action and representation. In this paper, I will first delineate three waves of Southern social movements, namely national liberation, anti-developmentalist, and anti-neoliberal movements, trace their dialectic interlinkages, and address their differentiated levels of success. To that end, I will shed light on one particular social movement of each phase and discuss how they contended with the prevailing status quo, their motivations, aims, and achievements. I will then argue that, as both the spaces and groups they represent and the structural mechanisms they oppose have become consolidated, deterritorialized, and globalized, we should reject the state-based North-South binary in favor of a cosmopolitan rearticulation of Marxist class antagonism that makes the transnational subaltern the centerpiece of both oppression and resistance. Thereby, I am endorsing the post-sovereign counter-hegemonic project which does not only recognize the inexorability of globalization but also the dialectic potential inherent in that fact.

Before tracing Southern social movements throughout the 20th century, it appears imperative to evaluate the relevant parameters of the essay prompt and their implications for my argument. I will define *social movements* in loose reference to De la Porta and Diani (2006, p.20) as social entities with differentiated levels of formalization and organization that aim to redress or champion political, economic, and/or social issues, and most often engage in conflictual relations to do so. Historically, *Southern* social movements are embedded in the postcolonial sphere, "which is simultaneously constitutive of and constituted by the dynamics of (…) conflictual encounters over the forms, directions and meanings of development" (Motta & Nilsen, 2011, p.3). As I will argue in later sections of this paper, however, not only has the subject of controversy shifted, the least in content and the most in form and context, the space in which these social movements are to be conceptualized, theorized, and championed has transcended geographical delineations. Rather than going down the rabbit hole of defining socio-political power, let alone evaluating it, I will simply consider the extent to which social movements in the Global South have been successful in achieving their aims. This paper is neo-Marxist in essence, as I emphasize the dialectic of historical materialism and its manifestation in class struggle. As social movements, and even more the socio-economic, political, and cultural structures they contend with, are vastly complicated phenomena, I am bound to make a decision regarding the perspective I choose and the conclusions that perspective can provide for. Thereby, I do not claim that my analysis is exhaustive and encourage further work to shed light on, amongst others, racial identity, culture, and human rights norms and how they build upon or can be related to my work.

Based on Motta & Nilsen (2011), three waves of Southern social movements can be identified that, while in part geographically, chronologically, and ideologically imbricated, were negotiated and carried out against variegated forms of structural oppression: national liberation, anti-developmentalist and anti-neoliberal social movements. What they have in common is their (primary) locus in the postcolonial, their philosophical indebtedness to (variations of) the Marxist paradigm, and their critical struggle against structural hegemony. They are to be distinguished, however, by geographical and historical contingencies, by the form of 'the beast', hegemony, and, in the case of the third wave, by the extent to which previous conceptions of territoriality gaze into space.

National liberation movements had been gathering momentum for a while already, but became a global, systemic force by the end of WWII. The power vacuum left by the devastations of war and the anti-colonial predisposition of the powers and institutions that filled it were conducive to their struggle for sovereignty and self-determination in the colonial world, which by then consisted predominantly of Africa and Asia. Their project was not as much the deliberate expansion of Westphalia, but the dislocation of colonial hegemony. As Seth (2002) points out, Lenin had provided a Marxist rationale for national self-determination by infusing it with the notion of anti-imperialism, and so, while there was pronounced variation, much of the first wave of Southern social movements was owed to the revolutionary spirit of the Marxist paradigm (see Wolfe, 2003, p. 110), from 'Portuguese Africa' to Indonesia and from Nehru to Nkrumah whose Constitution People's Party lead the Ghanaian independence project. After Nkrumah's CPP carried off a sweeping victory in the 1951 election which paved the way for independence six years later, Nkrumah told the press: "I am a Marxian socialist and (...) I am unalterably opposed to imperialism in any form" (Bourret, 1960, p. 176). As many other socialist, anti-imperialist national liberation movements the CPP and the syncretic Nkrumaist philosophy it is derived from, rejected the racialized colonial hegemony of the West and championed utopian pan-African self-reliance and self-determination (cp. McClendon, 1999).

As representations of the Westphalian subaltern, the colonies, national liberation movements like the CPP were successful in breaking the chains of formal colonial hegemony, although colonial remnants lingered on in epistemic and economic terms. In terms of championing the interests of sub-state subaltern groups and popular classes, however, Silver and Slater (1999, pp. 202-2011) argue that national liberation movements proved more bourgeois-nationalist than international-socialist, engendering not as much a radical social revolution as they instead constituted an updated reiteration of social hegemony, in which popular movements were repressed by the new power elites and in which the revolutionary anticapitalist challenge was contained. Murray (1967) voices similar thoughts regarding the Ghanaian project. After independence in Ghana, for instance, the United Party formed in opposition to the centralization of state authority only to be banned in

1964 when Ghana transformed into a one-party state. Motta and Nilsen (2011) take a more forgiving stance on the bourgeois-nationalist hegemonic project of developmentalism, an accumulation strategy which propagated national development through protectionist industrialization, and had been picked up in both decolonized Asia and Africa and long-independent Latin America in order to 'catch up' to the Global North. Accordingly, "the integration of popular classes into the struggles for national liberation broadened the scope of anti-colonial nationalism to incorporate subaltern demands for social justice" (p.5). Thereby, the developmentalist project gathered widespread support by wooing both the bourgeoisie that directly benefitted from protectionist policy and the popular classes, which, by virtue of the 'moral economy', became entitled to state services and benefits (developmental guarantees).

However, developmentalism as a hegemonic project did indeed reproduce exclusion and elite control to some extent, Motta and Nilsen concede, dividing the subaltern into two categories: the included subaltern that benefitted from the guarantees of the moral economy and the peripheralized subaltern that was excluded from the social contract of developmentalism. The differentiated experience of these groups in developmentalism ran roughly along four lines of division: formalization of labor, urbanization, gender, and race (as in Latin America and South Africa) or caste (India). The second wave of Southern social movements, then, was constituted by the mobilization and politicization of the peripheral subaltern, against the centralized power of the developmentalist state, finding expression in the rise of the popular left in Chile, Argentina, and Brazil, a repeated surge of radical national liberation against racial supremacy in South Africa and Zimbabwe, and struggles for sustainable, equitable, and accountable communitarian democracy in India. Like the Narmado Bachao Andolan (NBA) movement, for instance, which, amongst other things, rallied against the displacement of *adivasis* and environmental destruction in the Narmada Valley in Madhya Pradesh, these social movements called the developmentalist state out on its failure to meet its social obligations as well as demanded alternative forms of development (Nilsen, 2011; Souza, 2011). In its contestation of the central government's construction of large dams on the Narmada river, the NBA was able to mobilize the subaltern across caste and occupational boundaries but eventually failed to hold the state accountable to liberal institutionalist principles. To Nilsen (2011) that failure is emblematic of many anti-developmentalist movements which assumed the state to be the "most suitable conduit for subaltern emancipation" despite its function as "a key modality in the reproduction of fundamental structures of power" (p. 105).

Nonetheless, on a local and regional level, anti-developmentalist movements were important in renegotiating the economic and political terms of developmentalism, beyond that, however, as the NBA bears testimony, they were ultimately unsuccessful in shaping the trajectory of development in the postcolonial. Instead, transnational capitalist elites, stirred by the subaltern challenges to their class power, launched a neoliberal counter-revolution, which advanced "restrictive monetary and fiscal policies, a curtailment of (…) welfare programmes, tax reductions, privatization (…), and deregulation (…), spearheaded by the conservative forces that won political power in the West in the early 1980s" (Motta & Nilsen, 2011, p.11). Thatcherism and

Reaganomics constituted a turn from Bretton Woods-style embedded liberalism, which had at least carved out a space for national regulatory policy, to unfettered free-market neo-liberalism, undermining the developmentalist "institutional mechanism for economic redistribution and political mediation and consequently resulted in the disarticulation of the extant collective power of the popular classes" (ibid, p.12). The construction of neoliberal hegemony reified the class power of capital by facilitating the upwards redistribution of wealth and replacing developmentalism's logic of accumulation through state intervention with accumulation through dispossession of commons. The results were greatly exacerbated levels of intra- and international inequality, the precaritization of organized labor and the middle class, and the impoverishment of rural and indigenous subaltern groups. The establishment of a new legal order through supranational institutions like the WTO and the implementation of Structural Adjustment Policies through the Bretton Woods institutions helped edify neoliberal hegemony and fortuitous circumstances, such as the collapse of the communist block and economic crises in South and South East Asia, provided it with the opportunity to globalize.

As the nature of hegemony changed, so did the resistance. In consequence of fostering the deprivation of the informal subaltern and disempowering the organized subaltern, the transition from developmentalism to neo-liberalism reunited the previously divided popular classes, which came together to protest the newly formed neoliberal hegemony. This consolidation is less profound than it immediately appears, however, as the various subaltern groups' differentiated pre-neoliberal experiences still map onto their ideas regarding alternatives to the status quo. As Hardt (2002) reports, the World Social Forum 2002 bears testimony to the divisions within the anti-neoliberal realm of social action that roughly relates to two issues: 1. Who is the enemy? 2. What is to be done about it? One faction claims that the enemy really is the *globalization* of capital, demanding the reversal of globalization in favor of a reinforcement of national sovereignty and, in essence, the return to developmentalist state-led capitalism. As Hardt (2002) accurately observes, this camp consists largely of the subaltern included in the developmentalist project, which re-envisage the centrality of state power and the moral economy. On the other side of the debate, *capitalist* globalization is identified as the true affliction of the popular classes, and so alternative forms of globalization that transcend the capitalist logic are articulated. This stance finds largely support in the peripheral subaltern and Marxist-oriented organized labor. This internal debate is ongoing and it is too early to judge the success of the anti-neoliberal project altogether, but a few thoughts on both appear imperative.

Hardt's (2002) observation that status in organizational hierarchy (i.e. proximity to formalized power) appears to be positively correlated with support for national-sovereignty approaches to global neoliberal hegemony gives a first impression of why those might be inadequate to comprehensively represent the subaltern. Four more aspects deserve mention: Firstly, it should be kept in mind that there is no guarantee that the peripheralization of a wide array of the subaltern will not occur once again in a post-neoliberal developmentalist state just as it did in the pre-neoliberal developmentalist state, and that the reproduction of asymmetry and oppression will be averted this time. Secondly, interpreting Hardt's aforementioned observation with a critical perspective and empirical hindsight, it can be argued that returning to developmentalist projects premised on the primacy of national sovereignty is prone to despotism, as some of its most prominent advocates at the World Social Forum 2002, namely the Brazilian PT and the Venezuelan PSUV, have recently demonstrated. Thirdly, as Hardt & Negri rightly claim, "the logic of globalization is inexorable" (Seth, 2002, p. 565). Global neoliberal hegemony, or *Empire,* has deterritorialized and centered sovereignty and united "a series of national and supranational organisms (…) under a single logic of rule" (Hardt & Negri, 2000, p. xii, as cited in Seth, 2002, p. 566). Fourthly, and most importantly, not only has that logic already transformed the nature of social movements in the South and around the world, it harbors enormous potential for their successful pursuit. As the adversaries of social movements have converged into global neoliberal hegemony, a new form of solidarity has arisen that finds expression in a common struggle against it (Hardt & Negri, 2000). As neoliberal hegemony becomes increasingly transnational and augments subaltern spheres within the North and transnational elites within the south, social movements around the world have begun to graduate increasingly from territorial specification (especially vis-a-vis the North-South dichotomy). Transterritorial movements like LGBT rights activism, Kony 2012, Anonymous, or *Occupy* bear testimony to that development. In consequence, we are forced to reevaluate how we conceptualize and theorize the way in which the third wave of Southern social movements has transformed their character. The orthodox North-South binary is attempting to reify the antagonistic logic of Marxism, but as within that logic the history of society is a history of class struggle, it is more adequate to conceive of that antagonism not in monadic-state terms but in terms of the oppression of the global subaltern by the class power of capital and those that wield it (may that be the global bourgeoisie or as transcendental and abstract an entity as *Empire*) and of Southern social movements as struggles of resistance by the former against the structural hegemony of the latter. In that vein, speaking of subaltern social movements appears more appropriate and fruitful, as it recognizes that representation has become transterritorial and class- rather than state-bound. Especially the *Occupy* movement is not only a striking example of the anti-capitalist response to deterritorialized and decentered global neoliberal hegemony but of a transnational subaltern that is deterritorialized in its articulation of alternatives to development and the deregulated status quo. The *Occupy* movement emerged in September 2011 as a response to the instabilities and injustices of the global financial system and articulated an egalitarian agenda of social justice. First protests occurred in New York City and then quickly spread around the world with 951 cities in 82 countries just a month later including many versions in the 'Global South', especially in Latin America and (South) East Asia (Rogers, 2011). Through dialogue, deliberation, and civil disobedience it is "fighting back against the corrosive power of major banks and multinational corporations over the democratic process, (…) inspired by popular uprisings in Egypt and Tunisia, and aims to fight back against the richest 1% of people that are writing the rules of an unfair global economy that is foreclosing on our future." (Occupy Wall Street, n.d.). The *Occupy* movement does not only consist of the popular classes but also of precaritized and/or capitalism-skeptic segments of the middle class. Rather than being merely a representation of the physical subaltern, *Occupy* also gives voice to democratic socialist discourses that inhabit the subaltern as a philosophical space. As Stevenson (2014) points out subaltern social movements need not only represent the subaltern in the physical sense (representing individuals comprised in subaltern groups or classes), but can also represent discourses that emanate from the subaltern or depart from the status quo so radically that in themselves they are subaltern. Thereby, Stevenson expands the notion of representation in and through subaltern movements by transcending the representation of physical space and human experience to include the representation of the multiplicity of discourses that subaltern groups inhabit. In the particular case of the 'Bolivarian Alliance for the Peoples of Our America' (ALBA), Stevenson identifies a discursively representative function that beyond the attempt to "construct a constituency based on the malleable notion of 'the people'" (p.179), primarily gives voice to economically radical and politically progressive climate governance discourse (i.e. Green Radicalism). Her examination also reveals, however, that genuine representation needs to be a two-way process that ensures consistent dialogue between that which represents and that which is represented. Such a form of deliberative accountability then is crucial in discussing the question of legitimate or accurate representation and differentiating it from social movements like Kony 2012 that have been subjected to widespread criticism for speaking for rather than on behalf of the subaltern. *Occupy*, however, seeks to avoid that trap by making Habermasian discourse and deliberative dialogue the foundation of and method by which agenda and social action is constructed (Min, 2015).

As addressed before, globalization is not only inexorable but also full of dialectic potential for subaltern social movements. The transnational nature of *Occupy* bears testimony to that fact. As Hardt & Negri (2000) argue and as Seth (2002, pp.568-569) hints at, the deterritorialised reign of capitalism enables global counter-hegemonic movements that empower the subaltern multitude to transform capitalist globalization into a sort of globalized, cosmopolitan communism. Post-sovereign, alternative globalization approaches are therefore embedded in the Marxist dialectic of historical materialism, yet transcending its focus on the means of production towards the means of economic and political governance. Just as Marx championed capitalism's inherent potential for technological progress and the development of the means of production, for it would endow the material basis for socialist superabundance, so do anti-capitalist globalization movements cherish contemporary capitalism's inherent propensity for developing a global economic and political logic, because it endows the popular classes with the political and intellectual space for resistance and revolution.

Conclusion

In this paper, I have identified three waves of Southern social movements – national liberation, anti-developmentalist, and anti-neoliberal -, which evolved, in part, as responses to one anothers' success and failure, and continued to challenge and be challenged by the systemic dynamics in which they were embedded. While national liberation movements like the Ghanaian Constitution People's Party were successful in achieving formal independence, the developmentalist state that they, in part, gave birth to largely betrayed radical hopes of counter-hegemony by reproducing structures of class struggle and exclusion. Anti-developmentalist movements like the Narmada Bachado Andolan that formed as a result championed the immediate demands of the peripheral subaltern for representation and participation as well as challenged the epistemic premises of development. Yet, they were eventually overpowered by a neoliberal counter-revolution launched by a transnational bourgeoisie that utilized state power in the West to deregulate the international political economy and construct a neoliberal hegemony that has been expanding since. As global neoliberalism has exacerbated intra- and international inequalities, precaritized organized labor and the middle class, and impoverished the peripheral subaltern, resistance has sprung up all around the world (e.g. *Occupy*). In the face of the deterritorializing effect of global neoliberal hegemony or *Empire*, contemporary social movements increasingly transcend sovereign boundaries, and the North-South binary, and are well-advised to continue doing so, as to utilize the dialectic potential inherent in global economic and political structures. As the class power of capital continues to augment structural inequalities and to reproduce hierarchies of oppression on a global scale, mobilizing and politicizing the transnational subaltern is as auspicious as it is urgent. Notwithstanding the theoretical and practical limitations of sovereign anti-globalization approaches to *Empire,* it becomes increasingly necessary that a well-organized post-sovereign left (re)occupies the space, within which frustrations with global neoliberal hegemony are experienced and expressed, and does not leave it to the reactionary right, which is all too eager to invoke the spectre of despotism and exclusion. Seldom has this been more relevant than now.

Bibliography

About Occupy Wall Street (n.d.). *Occupy Wall Street*. Retrieved from http://occupywallst.org/about/

Bourret, F. (1960). *Ghana, the road to independence*. Stanford, CA: Stanford University Press.

De la Porta, D. & Diani, M. (2006). *Social movements: An introduction (2nd Ed)*. Malden MA: Blackwell Publishing.

Hardt, M. (2002). Today's Bandung. *New Left Review, 14*, 112-118.

Hardt, M., & Negri, A. *Empire*. Cambridge, MA: Harvard University Press.

McClendon, J. (1999). *Consciencism: The philosophy of Nkrumaism* (PhD Thesis, University of Kansas).

Min, S. (2015). Occupy Wall Street and deliberative decision-making: translating theory to practice. *Communication, Culture & Critique, 8*(1), 73-89.

Motta, S., & Nilsen, A. (2011). Social movements and/in the postcolonial: dispossession, development and resistance in the global south. In S. Motta & A. Nilsen (Eds.), *Social movements in the global south* (pp. 1-35). London: Palgrave Macmillan.

Murray, R. (1967). Second thoughts on Ghana. *New Left Review, 42*, 25-39.

Nilsen, A. (2011). 'Not suspended in mid-air': critical reflections on subaltern encounters with the Indian state. In S. Motta & A. Nilsen (Eds.), *Social movements in the global south* (pp. 104-131). London: Palgrave Macmillan.

Rogers, S. (2011, November 14). Occupy protests around the world. *The Guardian*. Retrieved from https://www.theguardian.com/news/datablog/2011/oct/17/occupy-protests-world-list-map

Seth, S. (2002). Back to the future? *Third World Quarterly, 23*(3), 565-575.

Silver, B., & Slater, E. (1999). The social origins of world hegemonies. In G. Arrighi & B. Silver (Eds.), *Chaos and governance in the modern world system* (pp. 151-217). Minneapolis, MN: University of Minnesota Press.

Souza, R. (2011). Three actors, two geographies, one philosophy: the straightjacket of social movements. In S. Motta & A. Nilsen (Eds.), *Social movements in the global south* (pp. 227-250). London: Palgrave Macmillan.

Stevenson, H. (2014). Representing green radicalism: the limits of state-based representation in global climate governance. *Review of International Studies, 40*, 177-201.

Wolfe, P. (2003). The world of history and the world-as-history: twentieth-century theories of imperialism. In P. Duara (Ed.), *Decolonization: Perspectives from now and then* (pp. 101-118). London: Routledge.

YOUR KNOWLEDGE HAS VALUE

- We will publish your bachelor's and master's thesis, essays and papers

- Your own eBook and book - sold worldwide in all relevant shops

- Earn money with each sale

Upload your text at www.GRIN.com
and publish for free